TRAMONTANA

T R A M O N T A N A
is the first major collection of Hugh McMillan's poetry. The author teaches history in Dumfries Academy, and received a Scottish Arts Council Writer's Bursary in 1988.

Some of these poems have appeared in the following publications: *Thames Poetry; Argo; Orbis; Chapman; Lines Review; Radical Scotland; Poetry Wales; The Glasgow Magazine; The Rialto; West Coast Magazine; Poetry Australia; The Listener; Prospice; InterArts; The Spectator; The Scotsman; Poetry Review* and *Triumph of the Air* in the series Envoi Poets, published in 1989.

TRAMONTANA

POEMS
Hugh
McMillan

D O G   &   B O N E
GLASGOW 1990

THIS BOOK WAS
FIRST PUBLISHED
IN SCOTLAND 1990
BY
DOG & BONE
PRESS
175 QUEEN VICTORIA
DRIVE, GLASGOW,
DESIGNED BY
ALASDAIR GRAY,
TYPESET BY
DONALD G. SAUNDERS
PRINTED BY
PRINTALL, CLYDEBANK,
BOUND BY
WM. ST. CLAIR WILSON

ISBN 1 872536 11 5

THE PUBLISHER ACKNOWLEDGES
SUBSIDY FROM THE SCOTTISH
ARTS COUNCIL TOWARDS
PUBLICATION OF THIS VOLUME

29/10/91

TO
MY
MOTHER

TRAMONTANA: (Adj.) from beyond the mountains ... foreign, uncivilised. – (n.) a dweller beyond the mountains; (in Italy) a wind from over the mountains, a north wind. With the connotation 'uncouth, unpolished, barbarous.'

– O.E.D. and Chambers

" ... it seemed more reasonable to regard all this as some mere transitory tramontana, some boreal thrust, yet it was most unfortunate for the roses."

– Anthony Burgess,
The Napoleon Symphony

TABLE OF

CONTENTS

THE PLOT UNFOLDS

When I looked out
it had stopped snowing and
no-one had made a mark on the day.

The schoolkids passing through
left a small preamble in the snow
and shopgirls, glumly following their feet,
made little dents with their shoes
till the street read like braille.

Half an hour passed.
A man shouldered his briefcase
and stamped along, each print
an improvement on the last,
and the road ran like a ledger.

Three pinstriped men underwrote it,
a girl running in high heels punctuated it,
and at the very end,
when I was guessing at the story,
some dogs added the very small print.

A VERY SMALL MIRACLE

A lamb was born near Dunnet Head,
tumbling in a yellow broth of legs
on the dark earth,
finding its feet just before
the brawling wind from the skerries did.

Nobody paid much heed.
The ewes were not easily impressed
by gyniatrics and two old women
talked on about tomatoes.
There wasn't even a farmer there
to count this a triumph for finance.

The dreaming lamb wobbled
on the lip of cool reality.
At thirty seconds old it had felt
the first rough edge of a tongue
and already knew that life
was not a bed of turnips,

at a minute
it was standing quite still
staring rudely at me,
as if it knew that being born
a sheep here
in these extremes of circumstance
was a very small miracle indeed.

GIANT IN REMEMBERING

He was the hand that filled the hollow places;
smoke hung in a grey pall round his head.
He soared; his stone face, carved in memory,
seemed to touch the skirts of clouds. His tread
made forests shake. He was the giant smile
that put the wandering world to bed.

He loved the storm.
On nights torn with fire he painted
mad seas and smeared
the skies with tongues of red
like lightning.

As years passed, they sometimes said
that he was ill; that his time shot down
alone and walking in the desert had crippled
him. He could revert,
become a danger. I knew better. Instead

the sun had filled his quick mind
with colours and only sometimes bred
a kind of blindness. Still, he left,
as leaves flaked and skeins of geese sped
south. Later, as I turned cold eyes
to loops of dark and winter sky,
they even tried to tell me he was dead.

THE SPANISH SOLDIER

Andrew has just come in, flashing us
an easy smile, the way he does when
he's got a half-eaten earthworm
in his fist or is wearing
the chicken as an overshoe.
This time he's carrying a
small figure he's unearthed upstairs.

The Spanish soldier has a fawn
uniform and forage cap. One of his arms
is severed at the elbow and he leans
cheerfully as if the missing hand
had once carried a suitcase of lingerie,
or good paperbacks, or a few
things packed for a High Life Break
in Rimini. His face, once tanned,
is chipped but it still radiates
a boisterous bonhommie.

I had a whole collection once,
mostly square jawed American types
with bazookas in their teeth.
They were a perfect fighting force,
ready at any moment
to turn on the cat, the neighbours,
each other, unburdened by any strand
of conscience.
All except the Spanish soldier.
Rifle slung, knees casually bent,
a smile playing on his lips,
he never fitted in.
He couldn't fire his gun unless
you held him off the ground
and he was just too bloody affable.
He spread disaffection in the ranks;

14

a wordless plastic form of pacifism.
We tried execution once, for cowardice,
but the Spanish soldier was made
of something very hard and wouldn't
break.

I though he'd finally bought it
in '69 with all the rest,
when we used home-made napalm
in the paddy field that was my garden.
Where's he been since then?
Some Peace Studies Seminar at Bradford
University, perhaps, or Berkeley,
California. Somewhere hot,
for his stoop is even more pronounced
and his leg has slightly warped.

Andrew's grinning.
He thinks he's found a new recruit
but I can tell, even now,
from the confidential way he's
bending over Darth Vader,
that the Spanish soldier has not,
in any sense,
lost his inclination to the left.

THE TRIUMPH OF THE AIR

I didn't know what gliding was
but I liked it:
while my father juggled hot geysers of air
high above the patchwork frazzle of Edinburgh,
I was left at my Gran's,
in a carpet like the ocean,
butting through squalls of wool and lavender,
past mahogany islands,
harvests of anemonies,
to the edge of the world
where doors boomed like cliffs
and continents of furniture tapered away
to snowfields of china cups,
and dust swam in hellesponts of light,
blazing like rubies.

Under a stool I could part the fronds
and watch the mariners
driven by undiscovered tides.
My Gran creaking with plates like an ironclad,
my mother billowing by in white.
I remember the last time.
There were sudden bells and shadows
and I was pitched out.
Hands plucked at me, faces soaked me,
I tried to swim but
like my father was drawn dizzily
towards the hard heart of the sun.

BAD NEWS ABOUT
SUICIDE BY DROWNING

When the world was too much
I went to Palnackie.
I had a notion to die there in a rockpool,
my profile pointing exquisitely out to sea,
but when I lay down
I was harassed by a gang of gulls
honking in stereo
and butting the air with their skin heads.
When *they'd* gone,
to crap on a telephone box
or stick the beak in outside the chippie,
the sea shambled up
and spat on my shoes like a dosser,
mumbling, "Bohemia no got a coastline, then?"
This was dry humour from
an unexpected source.
It cracked the waves up,
and they thumbed their broken noses
from the bay.

HOLIDAY SNAP

A tiny piece of North Berwick.
The glare of monochrome and grey miles
of sea like some Scottish steppes;
the deck chairs circled like wagons against
the wind, and in the foreground, one small
Mexican, sensibly dressed in case of sun.

I know him well, and his water bottle.
Even now I can feel the plastic on the bare
right knee. Below an extravagant sombrero
the grin cannot defy the years that
stretch like sand between us.

I can't begin to imagine the depth of his
happiness, frozen on film so long ago; what
it felt like to be brown sandalled on that
beach, on that day, wrapped in concern
and cardigans.

He is a spook, lost but for this one image,
pinned in time like some dead moth. I can
tell more from my shadow than from him,
with all his smiles.

ON THE POINT

John Gordon is dreaming,
unfurled like a flag on Ardtornish Point.
His family came here
on holidays, parking their lozenge
of a caravan near needle cliffs,
in the lip of the gale,
only a toehold, a stone jammed
in the wheel, from disaster.
He dreams of his mother, legs laddered in light,
who barred the debtors' door
and swept up the summonses in the morning
in a small green tray,

of his father, who used oils thick as thumbs
and left a black trail
like a comet's: the sharp spines
of paint rearing like beasts,
the photographs in Palestine
astride that great horse.
Lawrence of Dumfries.
Whatever faults or virtues the pair of them
had owned John had forgotten,
if he ever knew,
and pared down to symbol, to private myth,
they stare like Errol and Mrs. Flynn
from endless fields of Kodachrome.

John sniffs, as tiny boats hop
like sandflies in the slough of sea.
The more anchored he becomes,
the more he seems to see his wake,
the more he hears birds squealing
like chalk on the wall of sky
and sees the sun sweeping boys back for tea,
when they didn't need to dream of summer.

STONE LIONS

Swollen with salt
they hold their open paws
to the pulse of oceans
and the tide still beating
like a drum.

Tethered to the ribs of battlements
they guard comical tiers of stucco,
galleries teetering on stilts,
sloppy walls that stagger towards the shore
like a rabble and collapse
in the surf.

They keep a wary eye on bistros,
backgammon schools,
little houses held together with layers
of washing, some drunks,
a few German bikers making love.

If guarding this boozy lot
is an indignity, it doesn't show.
Every week, children put flowers
in the niches round their feet
and the lions, the last to think
there is something quintessential here
worth guarding, bare their teeth
and smile dreamily at the sea.

WAR GAMES NIGHT

Belgium, where in hell is that?
says the Czar, big Dan Gibson, as he moves,
knee deep in cardboard troopers, from
the Steppes. The Kaiser, a can of lager in his
hand, laughs and with an old ruler
moves files of Uhlans across the Lys.

Big Dan has little knowlege of the land
or the intricacies of the Schlieffen Plan.
He makes the conscripts walk in bare feet
from the Ukraine. He's lost the field kitchens
in Crimea. The artillery's in Vladivostock
while the gunners lounge about Kiev.

His peasants advance down the barrels of
the German guns and are reduced to pulp
Little piles of counters join the fag ash
and the empty bottles round the map.
Got you there you old bastard, the Kaiser
jokes, and big Dan shrugs.

Albert of the Belgians is at the bog and
Ludendorff is making toast. Only Dan is
at the board. Crowned in white smoke he is still
facing west. A million men, I hear
him muse, well well.

Through the window an August breeze moves
the distant skeletons of trees
and I am tempted to think of endless blood
on the Vistula when the likes of big Dan smile.

IN THE SOUTHERN GENERAL

My mother's on the fifth floor.
She's calm, though there's a dull
fire in her eyes and her hair is slick,
spread like a crown on the pillow.
"The cat's been missing you," I begin,
but she quickly interrupts.
"Grandmother came up last night.
She sat on my bed and played
the ukelele."
White as linen, I plump up
an encouraging smile.
"Mrs. MacDonald's sent some chocolate."
"Yes, I'll see her when I get downstairs."

My mother believes her world
has telescoped to a single
block of flats and that everything
she's ever known is stacked
chronologically beneath her bed;
her mother washing clothes
in Alt Criech,
Mrs Macleod reading to the class
in Gaelic from the Gospel
of St Mark and somewhere very close,
my sister snoozing in her pram
one sunny afternoon
in Morningside.

Her skin is darker;
thin and veined like leaves,
and she imagines herself suspended like
some delicate and drooping plant
high above her roots,
her life no longer a series of collisions.
of new beginnings, but a single line

you could trace with your thumb
or read like a sign outside the ward:
Down one flight for middle age,
Access by lift to infancy.

In my shaken state
it's a convincing tale:
all the people and places that made her,
here to see how she turned out,
to play ukeleles on her bedspread
at the end.
There's only one mystery left;
upstairs.
I think it's the Nurses' Home
but I don't push the point: I have no desire
to know what grim things lie ahead.
"Go up and have a look," she says,
cheerfully, as I make to leave.
"And bring us back some lamb chops."

THE STATION BAR

It's not the real world,
that's for sure.
Here are the stateless leaving,
and not all on the railway —
some are on a journey quicker than that.

No-one sees them off.
There's no colour or crying,
only a last sour mouthful of sunlight,
a kiss of ash,
a Daily Record kicked around all week
and waving, limply.

Trains surround them
shuddering like dreams
but they no longer think of sailing
along the cold rails.
This is Terminus,
and through the plate glass
travellers hurry past the debris of the day.

XMAS STORY

Numb windows
and spires through orange cloud.
In the fist of the day,
cottoned by frozen breath,
they pause,

three young girls in among the trams
and foreign lights, Christmas coming.
Under linked arms, gifts
in snakes of tape.
In the middle of the cobbled road
they stop and laugh,

On white sloped streets,
cool as prismed lights from strange stars,
they stop and laugh
and the snow, driven down
from rooftops,
will never sting their eyes.

WHO FARTED IN ROOM XIX?
(The Ufizzi, July 1988)

Ghirlandajo's Madonna has gone quite green.
It can't have been the Nuns;
zipped up tight in their white frocks
they are removed from this world by
high feats of tailoring.
Dresses stacked like sails,
they glide an inch above the ground
and their nostrils twitch in the airless room
with the aroma of another plane.

It wasn't St. Sebastian.
His nose is turned up with the pure
stink of sanctity.
The Americans have turned from measuring
the stigmata to stare at me.
I shrug. Too much insalata my shoulders
seem to say but soon I am alone,
left in no doubt as to the place
of flatulence in devotional art.

Nevertheless the fruity smell
has raised some points.
For with all that greasy food surely the
saints themselves must have been prey to
the occasional blast, in which case is
it not a holy act?
Probably the Council of Niceae ruled that
the Apostles did not break wind. Poor sods.
But then this room with its squeaky cartoon
angels and its dapper shepherds hasn't much
to tell us about the real world.
Dogma squeezes art flat.

I'm off to the Venetian Room, to see the
fat ladies. Give me pagan influences any time:
the smell of fart as well as flowers.

MARINA

When I surfaced,
bloated with towels, eyes wrung out
and pressed between my palms,
Marina was singing somewhere,
a song about the sea.

Waterlogged,
I could see the lick of oceans
and Marina's cave
damp with tellin,
hung with little combs
made from cuttlefish.
I was dumb but I could feel her fingers
butting through a tangle of hair,
see her breast move in coral.

Years went by.
Continents were drowned,
stars arced and sizzled out.
I said at last
"My ardour for you is such
that I will leave the shallow
world of men."
"Oh, that's nice dear"
she said, replacing the hairdryer,
"Do you want anything on it?"

TOMMY

He came to school each morning in a hearse
(The firm did undertaking and taxi cabs were scarce)
and every time sank deeper
in dirty coils of anorak
so it sometimes seemed that from the dark
you could only see his eyes smoking
behind the tinted glass and folded wings
of leather.

At first, when there was still a gleam,
he drove through the Estate
like a Sheik burnoosed in his limousine,
straffing the houses and the wastes
with those eyes
but as time passed he realised
that the funeral was his.

Tommy wore his scars with dignity,
defended his family,
his Mum and Dads,
liked animals,
loved History
and had an IQ of 153.

One Exam time in May,
with the school shaking each sunny day
like a mirage,
Tommy had his chance of a new life, his ticket
out, and told us where to stick it.
Inside he was already dead
and drew spiders on the page instead.

THE LOT

The garden is wild here,
but has not gone *back* to wild.
It is more darkly sinister than that,
cramped with atmosphere,
the plants fused and tangled as if
directed by a bleaker force,
like our own habits gone mad.

The flowers have crossed the line
to territory;
propriety has turned to greed.
Barbed like scimitars they gather
at the boundaries, chatter at
the broken teeth of fence.

Between the shattered brick and rust
are crippled stems, blind
to light, scales of livid ivy, huge
grasses drunk with size
and greasy rain.

The truth is our arrogance,
in tamest form, has bred this
terrible, familiar place.
Here is our future.

SALTY

My history teacher was an old sailor.
At school assemblies, numb with praying,
I would look up and see him
straight and sharp as a tusk,
a glower scrimshawed on his face.

No singing:
he didn't believe in God.
He balanced on the lip of the stage,
legs astride as if to catch the swell,
and scowled down his pirate's nose,
defying them to produce the source
of all this whingeing,

something as roaring as the sea,
or that Scandinavian wind
that howled through his teeth,
through the eyes licked by white hair,
and shivered our timbers.

His colleagues hated him.
They hinted at a weakness for boys,
whispered he was found at the end
in an indecent posture
(by some trick of pathology
clutching himself).

He was replaced by a man who ate Vick
and on a sepulchral Monday morning
God reclaimed his sea of bobbing heads
but I was at Salty's funeral
where thunder chuckled in the sky
and I saw the minister blanch,
drowned by a growl from the grave:

"Tell that bastard to stop talking
through his holy arse:
I died with a tiller
in *my* hand."

AN AMERICAN DREAM

Reading Bukowski,
drinking Michelob
and watching the sky
bounce away to the wide lapels
of the world
I was moved by a vision of America,
a pandemonium of blue and prairie gold
snapping past my eyes like film,
and I sniffed a freedom
born of space, or its illusion,
then the Guard announced "Kilmarnock,"
a sound like softly closing doors,
and when an old man asked
Is this us then? I had to say yes it was.

ANGLOPHOBIA

Sometimes, after ten pints of Pale in Mather's,
my pals and I discuss, with reasoned calm,
the origins of Anglophobia.

The philosophy was mother's milk to me.
Our cat was called Moggy the Bruce.
In 1966 my uncle Billy died on his knees
before the telly screaming "It didnae
cross the line ye blind bastard!"
I remember my Grandad, seventy five
and ridged with nicotine, sitting, grimly watching
a schoolgirls' hockey match. Hands like shovels,
he'd never even seen a game with sticks
but he was bawling "Bully up, Fiji,
get intae these English!"

An expression of lost identity, they say.
Some identity.
We were the most manic crew of cutthroats
out, never happy unless we were fighting,
preferably each other; any venue,
Turkestan to Guadeloupe.
It was only after the Pax Britannica
that any of us had a free minute between rounds
to contribute to the culture of the world.

By some strange alchemy we had however found
the untapped source of arrogance and up
to our arses in mud we could thumb our noses
at the Florentines and all the other poofs
of the Renaissance and take some solace
from thumpings by our betters by claiming
moral victory; a piece of turf from Solway
Moss and the crossbar from Culloden.

But despite all that, and sober, the limp
red lions stir the blood and in a crowd of
fellow ba-heids I'll conjure up the pantheon
of Scotland's past and jewel it with lies.
Unswerving stubbornness.
I suppose that in the graveyard of nations
Scotland's epitaph will not be a volume
like the French but a single line:
Ye'll be hearing from us.

TRAWLING MIDNIGHT

He had slowly turned the shade of
sinking hours, the arms dull and fading red,
the body angled, bent dark green
and daggered down to water.
Through tight eyes I watched him
anchored like a bronze,
diffused at last in night.

Folded in the bank I slept and
only once dreamed or saw him
through the splintered clouds. He was
rocking, pivoted between the planes.
Stars swum in the crook of one huge arm
and he trailed his circling line
through burning fields of light.

1990

En route to culture,
I am derailed in Kilmarnock.
The buffet is like some recipe for Scotland:
two labradors (crossed) in a reservoir of grease,
a drunk man swallowed by his toorie,
two infants drifting on a sea of broth,
seventeen pints of lager,
the tang of tar and sweat and beans.

The minutes shuffle by
and hours kick like fractious children
at their skirts.
The room has a strange and stygian appeal,
a kind of alternative panorama
for shortbread tins.
"Aye, there's strong beer in all of us"
an old boy says.

I have to agree.
It's 10 o' clock.
On the boulevards the pie shops
are opening
and wet leaves are brushing through crowds
to all the gutters of Glasgow.

WILLIE

"Drunk or sober,
yon man can pit a carpet boul
or a keystane right oan the button."
Willie is nodding modestly
in the Fleshers' Arms,
70° proof, if he's a day.

Willie doesn't age.
Like his dykes, he weathers.
He hasn't lost his hair,
but mislaid it in an absent minded way:
it's strung up there somewhere
on the rich topography of scalp
as thick as ever
but vitrified,
as impenetrable as his handiwork.

Below it, creases run
through the skin
like dry river beds.
There are hard callouses
round the smile
that defines and defies his history.

His face is a map
and like all landscapes
is variable.
Willie hasn't always been good.
I think he predates such concepts.
He is both sides of a very old coin.
The man *is* Galloway

NATURAL WASTAGE

Mid July, and the streets are dry
as dust
though in the wash of traffic,
the white shell of brick and glass
and the pavement that bubbles
in the distance like melting
butter, there is a hint
of water; a promise that the drought
will soon end.

In the same hope
the hunters are here,
in doorways,
on their backs in the scrub,
whistling through the belly
of the day. They're here
on the advice of their organs,
those blunt and rubber totems
long on instinct,
short on sensibilities.

In this paralysis of heat
the girls are leaving school
for good,
teetering on their long legs,
pausing to sniff the stale
and thrilling scent of predators
before they dart into the dazzle
of the crowd, the many limbs
like long grass waving,
and, long before any frontiers
are reached, the teeth.

MAJORETTES

There's a ragged science.
Batons flirt with gravity
and bounce beyond the probability of hands.
Teeth shuffle into line
and wink like semaphore.
Slow as sleepwalkers
the Lochside Leopards are probing
for rhythm in an overdose of base
while their brothers juggle with crisps,
leaving little mountains
for their mothers, erupting in applause,
to dust with ash.

The day isn't short of drama.
The Janitor's had his eye put out
and there's a rumour that
one of the Teeny Texans is Rumanian.
Her beard seems a clear
infringement of the rules.
The Committee will confer.

There is one girl
whose well schooled teeth are hidden
in a frown of concentration.
She catches and throws
and follows the flight of the wand
as it spins in the cobwebs
and the fractured light
and returns perfectly to her palm.

She stalks off in silence.
The Dumfries Marching Band Association rules
may be vague on transexuals
but they are explicit on those
whose horizons aren't low enough.

ACROSS THE BRIDGE

Bouncing across the river with Andrew.
A tattoo of legs, the shoes with the red
teddy bears slapping against my chest,
the gloves trailing like flags,
the fistful of hair and ribbons
of water through the spars of
the bridge.

It's getting dark;
there's light slipping through
the trees and, for a moment,
deep light in the bellies of clouds
and broken water, spreading around
us like fire.
Then Andy screams, a shrill sound like
a bird, and the shadows begin to gather,
like old men, in the park.

SATURDAY AFTERNOON IN THE GROTTO

Santa's in Sauchiehall Street.
There's a file of cheery white faced boys
with convict cuts and little oval heads like eggs
and bright red freckles,
as if someone had stood at the front of the queue
with a paintbrush, flicking it.

Their Dads, more used to snug bars than grottos,
are wheezing and stamping with the cold,
playfully cuffing ears,
sharing in the seasonal enthusiasm for chimneys
by smoking like them.
The result is a surreal and Scottish kind
of Christmas ambience

with rubber reindeer lurching drunkenly
through the fog
and tattooed men crunching, blind, through
polyester snow, scything down the penguins
and eyeing up the elf who's taking the photographs:
Give her a ride in my sleigh anyday.

It's happy enough
but I am a more modern father
so I was sad to see Andrew vault
like a paratrooper from Santa's knee,
pick a handgun from the box
and cock it jauntily at the girl behind the polaroid
as if to say:
*Not much call for the Spyrographs this afternoon
is there Doll?*

LOVE POEM

My love has gone.
Stars in the puddles guide her home,
the stinging rain on cobble stones.
Out of my sight she doesn't walk
but flies. Zodiacs bend in her wake.
She's pinned the moon on her shirt top
and trails her sooty feet on chimney pots
and where she's brushed,
the night is black as diamond dust.

My love has gone
in a blaze of cider, with ash and cheery
embers of song and life in a beery
blast of noise curling after her like smoke,
like fingers tugging at her coat,
till a taxi hijacks her,
bears her back along the straight and narrow,
where street lamps glower
and the wind's too genteel to tap on doors.

My love is gone but I can see her;
Time is asleep in the sweep of an arm
and the town shuffles back, blinking in the calm,
tired as a pensioner.

A MEMORY OF WARSAW 1943

There are three boys in the photograph,
hurrying across a dirt road
towards a truck.
Behind them is a soldier
whose face is hard;
from distaste at this job,
or at his prisoners,
I do not know.

It's snowing. Windows are white
with it. The boys have tied up socks,
double knotted, thick shoes,
coats and cardigans,
a canvas bag with one protruding
jumper sleeve.
They're smiling, and they're waterproof,
but neither state will keep them safe
where they are going.

What a contrast:
the care that against the odds
had wrapped them up that winter;
and the savagery that with the soldier's
broad restraining hand
already was descending
on their small grey heads.

A PRESENT OF A SUBMARINE

The day I got it
I was in a lay-by,
a knuckle of tar near Lugar,
and the sun against the green slopes
of farms was yellow like butter.
I was on the back seat and the submarine,
black, with working parts, from the
poshest shop in Edinburgh, was on
my knees. I remember an open
window, blisters of heat on the dimpled
upholstery and sweat on my neck
and legs.
He said it was only a joke
and she said not the type of joke
I ever want to hear
and then there was no more wash
of cars or birdcalls but silence
like a choir in my head.

I fingered the long snout of
the submarine, the conning tower,
the propellors that moved,
the lines sleek as fish.
That's it, it might as well be it
he said, and the door slammed,
and he strode into the grass like
a god decked in light
and when he swept his hand
in a final cutting motion down
I shook and let go of the cruel
prow at last
for the safety of tears.

THE ENERGY GAP

It's the end of term.
2E are plugged into terminals;
the circuit is complete.
Each head is swathed in wires like a Medusa,
cables sworl from the lights like vines.
The ghostly sound of jungle drums
fills the air, the distant throbbing base
of a dozen Walkmen.

Behind a rampart of adaptors
they sit, softly beeping.
Their faces are an eerie green,
though a flash of red,
a ricochetting laser or a spent
photon lance, glimmers sometimes in the dark
then dies. Is that a cicada
or the far off retro of a space
pod lost in the endless
plastic dark?

Now and then they dart out
like pygmies to ask for extension leads
or the odd bit of welding gear.
In the sun they blink at me
and wonder at how,
with no input from the mains,
I can still, occasionally, work.

VETERANS

Sepia: the day in
stained glass. A cat
asleep in embers and the smell
of drying coats and hats.

They never talk but through
bevelled windows watch
winter in the steaming wake of buses,
people flailing, caught

in liquid streets
fishtailing fast
in time. Some intrude,
brush coolly past

the old oak bar,
the pitted skin and dominoes.
And always with ice cold eyes
the old men watch the slowly closing doors.

LINDSAY AND SUSAN AT TYNE COT

Two up to the minute girls,
spiky hair and ra-ra skirts,
bopped through Belgium to Haysi Fantayzee
and found themselves
at the end of a tourists' day
in Tyne Cot.

They'd struggled off the bus
where many didn't – all miles merge in time,
all stops seem the same –
and as the wind rose
wandered through the graves,
small dark shadows
in a greater galaxy of white.

They fell quiet, and drifted.
Lindsay among the pale rolls of honour,
Susan before one simple stone:
A Soldier of the Great War.
Known unto God.

No name.
No face.
No hint of human story but
this boy reached out
and for a moment told of misery and mud
so sad a tale that Susan cried.

And as the bus revved
and friends hung out the windows
baying for their tea
the girls stayed long enough to write
Lindsay and Susan 1983:
words cannot tell.

THE BEST DRIVE HOME

The best drive home
was in a little car like a lozenge
while grey washed over the hills
and the scars of rivers
and I picked out the needlework of stars,
thirty six at least, before I dropped
against a window furred with breath
or my sister's sleeping
mohaired shoulder.

In the darkness, well known roads paled,
drained of reference,
and our way home was punctuated
by a shadow mythology of sight and sound.
Shoals of insects blanketed our lights.
Comic weeds caught big headed with rain
bent in our flickering wake.
Road ends opened up like tunnels
and trees swept past like wings
or trailed wet fingers to
brush against the doors.

Frightened to the point of ecstasy
I sat and rode shotgun,
pursued by the wild apaches of night,
ambushed by cars with eyes like coal,
while our engine ticked like a metronome
and the air filled with friendly licks
of smoke and a kind of talk
unknown to me, then or since,
but fused forever in moments like these
when the world seemed a strange
and hollow place compared with one
of its simple parts.

THE CAULSIDE CAFE

Under the plastic vines
and oilscapes, thick as your thumbs,
of the Planet Mars,
men are watching the sun as it proceeds
calmly to the rhyme of bells
past the tidemark of another mewing Saturday,
the empty cans, the puddles
and the windbags.

Some are still drunk.
They are anaesthetised
but can't bear the incision of the day,
others stare at their saucers
and long for the duff rationality
of beer.

Andrew and I eat our roll,
build our bricks,
and look at a bright swathe
of Sunday in Dumfries,
a puzzle not quite in place.

MAY REVISION

Answers. Remember there are three,
one each from sections A and B
and one from those or Section C,
though that one could be
hard I reckon.
May Revision,
the long days beckon.

Write lucidly, remember.
Fill the page.
Be sure to know where
dates apply. Gauge
the time. You know the drill,
and can see the sun
spark clouds of broom on dreaming hills.

Remember Sarajevo. Who can say
the province that it sat in,
the time of murder, month and day
and the name of the assassin?
Alison, you know better than to chatter
and stray to thoughts of love
or sex, and things that really matter.

Hard work, remember.
That's the way you all succeed.
Don't you dare
relax. Or heed
friends that do. And class,
don't dance on old chalk paths
or run stark naked through the grass.

Remember this, one last good luck.
Take two pens
and if you're stuck
move on. And if you've sense

move on, forget the lot.
Do your May Revision
in an older school of thought.

BIRTHDAY GAMES

End of term assembly
and the Christians have no chance.
It was all over when the Rev's
flies came down
but now the Scripture Union, dressed as punks,
are drawing analogies like teeth
and the children stamp like Zulus
and pray for songs about conception,
which they know is rude.

I came in and a rich brew,
a warm hocus pocus of fart and mumbles and feet
steamed up my specs
and I could hardly make out our Angela,
the bonsai Brightman, stretching
in the mistletoe for notes.
Then Jamie dropped his silver
and was detained.

But this is a sort of exultation,
a nae nonsense kind of Scottish Christmas,
and I know where Jesus would be:
down here among the Romans,
if he could stand the smell.

THE MEDIUM AND THE MIXTURE
Hole in the Wa', September 1986

This is not the Place Pigalle
but there are paintings here
in the curl of smoke, in the tints
and halo of light,
in the texture, thick as oils,
stale as cigarettes, old as wrinkles.
Three hundred years of drool have
made this place what it is. And
droolers; for this is a return
to childhood, to mouths, sucking
on glasses, ranting and smooching
like madmen muted by the world but
free in a raw sea of words till
darkness pulls the shutters down
and the last spilled sounds are wiped up
like drink from the bar,
and they shuffle out, soft as a
mumble, pure as babies,
every colour in the rainbow
but always brown as beer.

Some doomed civilisation lives here
and they behave as if each drink, each
belly laugh, is the last, wrung by sorcery
from the suffocation of days.
Old men with skin like vellum grab
your arm, catch your eye,
as if they believe they will not die
if they are talking.
There are some not so much washed up
as out of step; eccentrics to a narrow
fringe of saintliness, dreaming
aloud with words and fooling no-one.

Enjoyin' yarsel? drawls Canada in his
star spangled shirt, tales rich as maple,
plenny of action dawntown.

Max is elbowing life into the accordion
and Canada jerks down the bar,
his hat cocked like Fred Astaire's,
his cuffs wet with whisky,
mouthing some Québecois river song
he's learned on some sore and sober
morning at the library.
In the hard light from the dart board
his face is full and yellow
like a doll's.
There's no wine bar neutrality here.
We're one step from the charnel
house or one step from grace.
We know the score.

ECHOES

In the television room with 5S.
Brown panelled walls, crisp packets
stuffed in the cracks like garlands
and narrow fingers of sun.

There's nothing to stir their emotions
in these images flickering across the screen,
the crushed skulls, the mud, the cratered fields
of crosses, safe in sepia.
There is a cosmic gap between these young
folk and mine, not expressed in
a mere seventy years of time.
They are history, these characters in
Charlie Chaplin brown, comically removed
from the technicolour world,
and they are television, where suffering
is daily pared to something else.

The programme ends. Frowns give way
to talk of Morten Harket and
cocktail hour at Valentino's.
Yet Jill and Stewart and the rest
are not insensitive. They just can't
see beyond the fun, beyond the sun
of this Spring day, and here, at last,
with these ghosts on film, is common ground.

SATURDAY IN THE WESTERN BAR

The Western Bar is the world pared
down to beer.
When you strip away the layers
of the afternoon like an onion,
the film of spray
arching from the wheels of buses,
the shoppers bubbling at
doorways, the smooth
sound of Desmond Lynam
on a score of distant television sets,
there is always a bitter core
like this, who sit in the shadows
and the wallpaper spined
with nicotine,
flopping like dolls on their
tall stools, tumbling soft
as babies and spilling
along the long bar like beer,
or sitting, bit parts
in a never-to-be-discovered film,
spitting words like glass
from bruised mouths and winking
at the go-go as, through gauzed
and ribboned light, the girl
on the slab turns
like meat.

MAKING FOR ARCADIA

Greece was on my mind yesterday:
the stabbing blues, the bustle
like a sea to drown in.
I caught the Picadilly Line to Heathrow
and the hiss of closing doors
was like wind in the cypresses
and my head bent dreamily to the warm
water prospects of the world
as if to a kiss.

At Hounslow I woke up
and the sky had darkened to a sweeping
crown of black. Rain pawed at the glass.
All the square jawed backpackers
had gone, spirited away, and, framed
in yellow light, the travellers were
a shabby frightful crew, huge bellied,
toothless, careering together like
the damned as the train juddered
screaming through a nightmare
of clouds, and leaves like hands
slid away from windows.

At the back, dressed in baggy trousers,
a bearded man gripped one of the spars like
a rudder. Light broke beneath his
steering arm and his cheerless
skirling laughter echoed through
the carriage as if through
endless hollow vaults.
Typical of Lunn Poly
not to tell me there was a stopover
for the over 30s.

HOME

Tall willowherb,
glum sentries of the wasteground,
crane their necks
and gawk like bored boys
outside the chippy
or the sodden Saturday crowd
waiting for the results
in long shop windows beaded
like curtains with rain.

There's a fine drizzle.
It fits like an old coat,
muffs the ears,
films the eyes.
It never soaks you,
but dilutes the senses
till all you hear is a low rush
of noise like spray
and all you see is a grey institutional
sky and the pale ghost of a sun
swinging somewhere like a spent bulb
or a night light to lull
us all to sleep.

Worst of all there's you,
with your hand waving bravely
from some train full of cans and ash,
the 14.20 detritus special dragging you
back on your tanned heels
to your roots.

LEAVING SCOTLAND BY TRAIN

It's not easy.
Near Perth there's a conspiracy
of gravity and guilt
that propels me forward in my seat
to squint at my motherland
from a foetal position,
my nose snorkelling through the coffee
and the world whirling backwards,
disappearing gaily down some Scottish plughole,
an Omphalos near Denny
where the land is conjured back
with all the sheep and the seagulls and the trees
still buttoned on it,
and broken down to formless green.

I daren't open my eyes
in case it's really done the trick
and I'm bobbing like a peeled lychee
in the gynaecological soup,
a heart pulsing in my ear and a gentle voice saying:
"Where do you think you're going, you bastard?
Stay here. Where it's warm."

BARRHEAD

New graveyards are bald,
the grass peeled back like skin
on a white skull,
scars still bleeding clay.
They are stark,
time has not drooled on them,
made them part of the warmer landscape,
grief has not been archived.
Mourning is too soft a word.
Here there is keening

and all our nerves on show.
There, they are visiting the dead by car,
cruising the gravel paths and peering at the slabs,
a kind of Drive-In Golgotha
And there a gravedigger dancing to Deff Leppard,
while his pals sprawl on the bonnet of the truck

And there. On the wet hill
cramped like an emporium,
an old lady is weeping
at the foot of a cross and it is
white and empty as a bone.

TEN PAST ELEVEN

Dickie's Bar.
Faces round as hops.
It is just after Eleven
and they are staring shyly at their drinks,
as if they had just been introduced,
or can't bear to remember last night's
passionate affair.

Outside, roads twitch by
like nerves,
cars nag, kids scream,
clouds fold over the sun
then unfold, like impatient arms.

Silence, for they are savouring
time with each thick mouthful,
drinking minutes.
Each belly talks of hours and days,
brags like a sailor about time
marooned from the world
in this land
where only the clock reminds,
tapping like a knuckle on the glass.

ALL AT SEA

The brown soaked bar,
smoke curling
on wet windows.

They are uniquely here.
There is no chemistry
like this elsewhere
or talk as racy.

Blown to diverse ends,
here, at last, for hours,
they ride the tide
and trade their tales

and when the door creaks
and cold seeps in
with the gannet calls of babies
or the distant roar of cars

like waves on needle rocks,
they huddle closer, laugh louder,
and the old salts smile.

OPEN DAY NIGHT

Forging south
while the storm snaps at our heels
and cars drift by on tongues of spray.
In the slough beside the motorway
lorries are anchored to flat vistas
of grey and green.
The road has drowned
and in a monotony of rain
we are becalmed
while trees and buildings slip by,
filling with wind like sails.

Near Crawford the bus gives up.
Willie gets out to blow down the tubes,
scrape away the callouses of brine,
coax it that final thirty miles.
Near a knot of workmen
brown with engine oil
I unload our cargo of schoolgirls.

In sight of these sleek and wiry men
with eyes like hot rivets,
starved of female company
since they were marooned here
at breakfast,
the girls light up like lamps,
unload the morning's intellectual suet
like mad balloonists cutting ballast loose.
They are alive.

The bus coughs to a kind of life
and heaves away from the racks of tyres,
the dead plants, the trellis work
like rigging,
Willie and I laughing like old salts,

too loud,
and the girls in the back
quietly dreaming of the sea.

REMEMBRANCE

In the mist,
slowly peeling over wet trees
and the piping birds,
they are remembering.
A dozen balding men
shuffle to salute.
Their breath steams away,
more solid than the memory.

In Lovers' Walk, warm with
full years' stone and fleeced,
red meated, with wine or
the stubborn touch of Brown Ale,
still after all these burgessed years,
they are remembering. But not war;
only dreamy cameraderie,
boys with eyes like ice.

THE LAST TIME

The last time I saw you
there were yellow clouds
between the spires
that ringed the Old Town
like teeth.

There was a gap
between loops of weather,
while tourists hedged their
bets in cafés,
and only two girls were
on the street, sprinting back
with lunch in the grey
wash of buses,

and even that sound
soon drained away. We walked
through quiet minutiae,
the layers of diluted light,
the wet wood,
the smell of coats,
while the skies hung fire
and cake-forks paused in space.

Then you walked off
and the rain began to bounce
ankle-high on cobblestones;
an opening at last
for umbrellas.

THE CHINESE GARDEN

When the sun plods home
and the ragged clouds swing behind it
like the hem of a tatty dressing gown
to snuff the light,
tiny trees beard its face
and their branches trail like fingernails
in folds of red and eggshell grey.

It is a mystery, this garden of lace
and fretwork trees,
a challenge to our muddy notions of November
and for a while we can forget
the juggernaut screetch of Scotland
on its daily rush to pandemonium

and watch children in a dazzle of grass,
building little towns of stone
while leaves shake with breeze like breath
and birds fly slowly
between the purple lips of hills.

SUPERVISING S3, SCIENCE

I'm high above Dumfries
on a bleached spur of high technology
while the town leans
in a haze of chimneys and towers
like minarets and collapses, at last,
in a ruin of Aegean blue.

I sit in my old sandals
weaving nets from threadbare words,
out of habit – few fish find their way
into these traps any more –
while the girls wade ashore
through the heat like Gods,
skirts tied around their strong thighs,
their skin tanned and faces
hard with light.
They have reduced the world
with their terrible eyes,
melted frontiers,
and they hold truth cooling
in their palms like ore.

Sarah breezes through the books,
the scripts scattered like totems
round my desk.
She's carrying a wire pot
that she's plucked from the ceiling.
I am still trying to understand
how a light bulb works and Sarah
is swinging at arms length, with
a matey carelessness, the structure
of the physical universe, the key to life itself.
It doesn't look like much;
a mesh of plastic balls.

I wouldn't have thought it would
hold a lobster, never mind
a generation.

ON THE SOLWAY

Cloud like a fist
in the throat of the sky
and the mouth of the sea
opens,
swallows
at the ragged shoreline of land
and the shells that rattle
like a boneyard at the flex
of its arm
and its salt sweat.

From the sea's green memory,
deep as the drowned,
it has thrown up on the sand
some blind effigy
that sprawls in the shallows;
spittled
rat tails of seaweed hair
and scallop eyes.
It has black drums
for legs
and a barrel
like bleached and gaping ribs.

It shifts disjointedly
with the tide,
like a broken body,
like the white viscera
of a mutant child.

MORE THAN GEOGRAPHY

I'm juddering through arteries of rock.
Going home is more than geography:
It's tracing the outline of a well loved face
with the fingers, again, of a child.

Water threads the scalp of hills
and soon we'll tip down to Oban
where the boats are set like buttons
on the belly of the bay
and every pavement used to lead to jam
or little fists of shingle where you could skim
a stone all the way, it seemed, to Kerrera

and where the *Columba* came
bringing back the half drowned
with their sodden duffle coats
and scarves like pennants
home to the warm,
butting in that last mile through the Sound
while clouds closed like eyelids over stars
and a piper faint as a gull
in the roar of the night
played us home, over all the muscles of the sea.

THE END OF THE ROAD

How can the road end?
There's no more tar, that's all.
This last town in Scotland is no terminus,
the road runs gently into the sea
as if it was the most natural thing
to drive on to Norway, or to Labrador.

Over Lerwick, bent like an ear on the coast,
the gulls hang, their bone heads
set against gravity,
willing fat boats home down
the throat of the day.
Like the doors,
the people have no locks.
They are raw, but distance
has not rendered them quaint.
The morning news – *Clothes line near Tingwall*
catches fire, a child's best jumper is burned –
doesn't make me laugh but rage
at all the other headlines in the world.

Oh what a breath of fresh air
is in these draughts from the north.
This is how we might all have been,
if we could have turned our backs,
if our nerves hadn't developed
faster than our heads,
if our eyes had been open to the sea
that beats like a heart here
even beneath the skin of the land.

IN ALL MY PUFF

My Puff: as nebulous as that.
The wicker man that flat breath
pumps like wind in white
ghosts of grass;
pith, meat, nuts and bones
that pop and wheeze;
the bad gas and gristle.

Beyond the belching fabric
is even less of bulk.
The things that ferment
from life, abstract to the
point of fizz: love, the
exclusive gist of
tastes and sounds.

So as to substance?
In all my Puff,
a phantom footprint
in a few mind's eyes
and the odd fart against
prevailing winds.

GENERAL

LORD BYRON'S RELISH
The Regency Cookery Book
by Wilma Paterson.

*" ... perhaps the best contribution to gourmet literature since
Gunter Grass eulogised the humble potato."*
—Ian Bell, THE OBSERVER

£7.50 (pbk) ISBN 1 872536 02 6

A SENSE OF SOMETHING STRANGE
Paranormal Investigations
by Archie E. Roy.

*" ... can only prompt wonderment and question in the reader
with an open mind."*
— Susy Dale, THE OBSERVER

£7.50 (pbk) ISBN 1 872536 06 9

THE ABOVE ARE AVAILABLE FROM:
Bookspeed, 48a Hamilton Place, Edinburgh EH3 5AX
031-225 4950

OR DIRECT FROM:
Dog & Bone, 175 Queen Victoria Drive, Glasgow G14 9BP
041-959 1367